SUCCESS IN THE LAUNDROMAT BUSINESS

A how-to guide for beginners

William Arthur

CONTENTS

PREFACE

I got the idea for this book from several of my customers. Many had shared with me that they also wanted to take the plunge and buy an 'easy' business like a Laundromat. I had one say to me "Look at you. You hang out all day talking to people and playing on the internet. All you have to do is take the money to the bank when you leave"

If they only knew. I decided to write this book to share what I've learned and to help anybody who is considering the laundry business to make the right choice based upon real world experience.

Additionally, I decided to share the exact methods I used to build my business. They may not all work for you. Maybe you have ideas I didn't think of. The point is, I hope to save you some time and money by sharing what worked and what didn't for me.

I made a few mistakes when I bought my first Laundromat. I was anxious to get the deal done and didn't evaluate as thoroughly as I should have.

Everything eventually worked out but it took two years longer than expected to hit my initial cash flow bench marks and projections. The timeline could have been shortened but I just didn't know what I know now.

Starting up a laundry business is a bigger financial and emotional commitment than many people realize. It is not simply a matter of putting in the machines and collecting quarters.

You will want to weigh your decisions as carefully as possible, consider all the options and be aware of potential downfalls. This book is intended to help you do just that.

CHAPTER 1-WHY A LAUNDROMAT?

All Cash, Passive Income Business

Owning a coin-op Laundromat is a proven way to make money without putting in the long hours associated with so many other types of businesses. It is the type of business that can, should you manage things properly, give you the flexibility and cash flow to pursue additional interests and opportunities whether those are other businesses or a quality leisure time.

Laundromats are similar to vending businesses in the sense that you do not have to be 100% present every day. You can, potentially, earn money 24 hours a day while only being present for a very small portion of that. The major benefit with of a well-run Laundromat is the ratio of time spent to money earned.

Here are the reasons why you should consider owning a Laundromat per CoinLaundry.org.

-Providing a basic necessity. Everybody washes clothes. The Laundry business was considered essential in most States during the Corona Virus Pandemic in 2020 and many remained open for business while other business owners were shut down.

-Weekly repetitive business. Most of your customers will be regulars from a within a one mile radius.

-No receivables-all cash paid up front. You get paid every single day you are open.

-Very little cash tied up in inventory. Vending machine items and wash/fold supplies are your inventory costs.

-Stable industry for many years.

-Simple to operate (but not easy).

-Good cash flow and ROI in comparison to other small business endeavors

-Conducive to multiple store operations

-Able to operate part-time.

And some reasons why not to per CoinLaundry.org.

-Large Capital investment required. This is particularly true if you build a new facility.

-Financial risk associated with large Capital investment. More so if the investment is financed.

-Rising operating costs (rents and utilities). Both go up every single year. You will need a strategy to raise prices accordingly.

-Competitive in many markets. Some areas may be oversaturated for this service.

-Scarcity of locations/stores for sale

-Impacts on Lifestyle. You do need to open and close the facility daily or arrange for someone to do so. Calls for assistance invariably come when you are engaged elsewhere.

-You wear all the hats. As with most small businesses, it's all on you to make it work.

-Repairs can be expensive if you are not mechanically inclined

-Personal Safety removing cash.

CHAPTER 2 - BUILD NEW OR BUY EXISTING?

Plan Your Escape Before You Strategize What And How To Buy

> *– "Begin with the end in mind." -Steven Covey <u>Seven Habits of Highly Effective People</u>*

> *- "If you don't know where you are going, you will wind up somewhere else." -Yogi Berra.*

This may seem strange to discuss how you are going to get out of the business while you are just now considering getting into it. But it is a critical part of your business planning that most people tend to overlook.

Generally, it is not a good idea to get into something without knowing how you will be getting out of it.

What Are Your Goals And Expectations For This Business?

"I will buy this business, work it myself every day for 25 years, then sell and retire"

"I will buy this business as an investment. All net profit will be re-invested elsewhere."

"I will improve this poorly run business, create value, sell for a profit within 5 years, then look for another".

Knowing how it ends will help you prioritize your decisions and keep you focused during the course of your ownership. You will over the course of your ownership ask yourself: Should I upgrade my equipment? Remodel the store? Take on a new service? The answer lays in how that action fits in with your escape plan.

The good news is, when you are ready to cash out, Laundromats tend to have a ready pool of buyers. They are much easier to sell than many other businesses.

How Is Your Mindset?

Operating a Laundromat is very much the same as running any other retail operation. Customers will spend a considerable amount of time in your location, and they want to feel comfortable. If you and your staff welcome them, answer their questions cheerfully and listen to their life stories, they'll come back. When you decorate the store, keep it clean and the machines in working order, so that customers will choose your location over the dingy place around the corner with the 'out of order' signs.

In short, the more effort you put into your laundry business, the more you'll get out of it, financially and personally.

The industry is what experts describe as a "mature market". Save for areas that are seeing a high population growth, pretty much every area that needs a Laundromat has one- or two or three that are competing vigorously. In some areas of the country, there are already too many Laundromats.

There is, however, room for new laundry owners. Many get into the business by purchasing an existing Laundromat and renovating it. Some also find that they can build a new laundry in an area with competing laundries and thrive by offering a bigger store, more services and better customer relations.

The coin-operated laundry industry needs to undergo a revolution. Too often the neighborhood Laundromat is dingy, unsafe, boring place that customers must endure on a weekly basis. It is often unattended and machines are out of order.

The decision to buy or build a Laundromat is a matter of your financial resources and the availability of desirable locations for sale in your target market. Many of the available units are smaller (1200 to 1500 square feet) and have older equipment. Newer locations are generally bigger, have updated equipment and generally appear cleaner and safer.

Given the choice of a brand spanking new business versus an existing location with sales history, you have some factors to take into consideration.

Either Laundromat should be in an area surrounded by apartments on a high traffic street as the majority of the customers that will come to your store will live within a mile of the Laundromat and the majority of them live in apartments. There should be plenty of parking, preferably with a very short walk to your door.

Most successful Laundromats are in a small strip center with at least one eatery or restaurant. Donut and coffee shops are best but imagine how customers will be spending their waiting time if not spending all of it in your Laundromat.

Rent Vs. Own The Building

You may have the option of purchasing or leasing a stand-alone space. This decision is based on similar criteria as owning or renting a home.

These criteria may include:

Is this a laundromat a long term (more than 10 years) commitment or a flip?

Am I sure or unsure of the location? Is the total leasing cost less than the total owning cost or vice versa?

It is best to own, in my opinion. Discuss the tax implications with your financial professional.

In simple terms, the Laundromat itself is your cash flow and the Real Estate is your Equity Growth. Your business will be worth much more after several years of Real Estate appreciation.

Should you rent, take great care in evaluating your Lease. As a general rule of thumb, a rent of more than 20% of Gross Revenue should try to be avoided.

Talk to your prospective new neighbors in the shopping center. Ask them what their rent is. Some will say-some won't, but any information you can get to negotiate with is priceless. Had I done this when I took over my first lease I would have saved myself hundreds of dollars a month when I really needed it at start up.

The lease is one of your largest monthly expenses and will be a significant factor in your business opportunity. The terms of your remaining lease and the willingness of your landlord to renew will have significant impact on the value of your business should you decide to sell.

Try negotiating for rent amounts that remain flat for the first 5 years. Leases of 15 years or more (including all options) are good as you need to have a chance to recapture your investment and make a decent profit for your efforts.

Building A New Laundromat

Getting into the laundry business with new construction will require a significant initial investment. The average cost at time of this edition (not including owning the Real Estate) is about $500,000. Therefore, it is essential to do your market research before committing to build a new Laundromat.

You must evaluate any existing facilities within a 3-mile area.

That includes any apartment building facilities and college dormitories. Ask yourself the following questions:

At what capacity are they operating?

What is the condition of the facility and machines?

Are any of your future competitors for sale? Why?

The answers to these questions will help you to determine if there is sufficient demand for another facility, where you can provide better service and approximate your future customer count.

I would highly advise AGAINST buying/building a new Laundromat UNLESS

: You have experience in the industry

: You recognize a truly underserved area

: You have the opportunity to own the building the facility will be in.

Make very sure you can obtain the proper permits to include sewer usage prior to committing as new permits can be difficult to get in some areas.

Pro's To Building A New Facility

It will reflect your design and vision

You will have the most up to date equipment

The location was handpicked by you.

Cons

The location is unproven

No existing cash flow

Possibility of permit denials/delays

Laying Out The New Facility.

The space has to have proper flow. Design your location with the assumption that every machine will be in use all day. Given that parameter, does the traffic flow properly and does every body have a place to work and sit?

You want your washers and dryers opposite each other. For example, if your Laundromat is long and narrow, you want to put all your washers on the left and all the dryers on the right (or vice versa). If you have an island of machines intersecting the location, have the washers in the middle and have the dryers line the walls.

It is always best to confer with your equipment distributor. They have years of expertise and will help you to determine your best equipment mix and layout for your specific location.

Try to have an even mix of size/capacity for your washers. If you have room for twenty washers- have five 6x, five 4x, Five 3x and Five 2x front load washers. Substitute two top loaders for two 2x front loaders if you insist on using top load machines.

Have at least two more dryer pockets than you have number of washers. Dryers typically run about twice as long as washers and that is where you will have your work flow crunches if operating at full capacity.

Double stack dryers are usually 3x capacity. Persons using the 4x and 6x washers will need two dryers for each load. A twenty washer store should have at least 22 dryer pockets, more if you can fit it.

Buying An Existing Business

Evaluating a business is a book series of its own. I will give you a summary of how I do it, but please seek trusted and qualified counsel to evaluate any deal before you sign.

A Laundromat will typically be listed for 3-5 times net earnings. This is way too high unless laundries are scarce in your area or the location is grandfathered for permits that are no longer easy to get.

I use two methods to determine a fair price. Replacement and Cash flow.

The Replacement method is comparing the asking price of the existing laundromat to the cost of building a similar one. The lower the asking price is in relation to the new build cost, the better the deal.

Deduct from your offer the replacement cost of any non-working machine. Partially deduct for any working machine that is over 5 years old as the life expectancy of modern commercial washer bearings is about 7-10 years.

The Cash Flow method evaluates the Income Statements and Profit and Loss Statements. Using this information, we can predict with a bit more certainty if the business, in its current state, will let you execute your exit strategy. I stress current state as you do not pay the current owner for improvements you will make to marketing and operations. 'Potential' is not a payable line item. Neither are tax deductions such as Depreciation. What matters and what you are paying for is actual cash that will be hitting your account.

The revenues from the existing operation must enough to finance the terms of your deal. The business has no value if it is losing money. Should this be the case and you think you can turn it around, offer to take over the lease and negotiate any outstanding equipment debt that has a lien.

The value of a profitable business is....... How much are you willing to pay for the revenue stream provided? Can you get a better return on investment (ROI) elsewhere? Your offer should reflect the cash flow the business provides in relation to the return on investment you are seeking.

If the business has a net profit of $100k, the asking price is $300k and the equipment is all working and under three years old is it a good deal? That's up to you. But my opinion is a 33% return on investment is a pretty good deal.

If the business grosses $100k, is losing money, the equipment is 5 years old with $10k outstanding lien and they are asking $75K? Probably not a good deal. This deal I would look at where I could shave expenses, improve service and determine my best price. Then offer to pay the balance of the equipment loan and take over the lease for the business if my improvements might generate enough to meet my exit strategy.

Evaluating Machines In An Existing Location

The expected life span of most commercial front load washers and dryers is about 10 years. Top load washers will last about 7 to 10 years. These numbers can be improved with proper and regular maintenance as well as educating your customers on proper use.

It is very important to verify the age of the machines you are buying and estimate when you will need to replace them.

Old and run-down equipment accelerates the need for expensive upgrades. Your maintenance costs will also increase until you do upgrade.

Operate each machine in the facility to ensure they work properly prior to purchase.

For washers, listen for any kind of grinding noise especially during the spin cycles. This could indicate bearing issues which are very expensive to repair. Also verify that all cycles (wash, rinse) provide new water to the machine. Failure to do so means the valves or computer board need replacement.

Inspect the plumbing. Look for signs of excessive corrosion or leaks. Test the shut off valves when the washers are in operation to verify good working order.

For dryers, verify consistent heat levels during the cycle on all setting (hi, medium and lo). Common problems that you may find with poorly operating dryers are:

- Dryer ignites, then shuts flame at temperature, fails to reignite to maintain temperature
- Dryer won't ignite
- Dryer only works on one setting
- Dryer wobbles or makes scraping sounds

These are all fixable things but those costs should be a factor in your offer price.

Don't be shy about asking for maintenance records from the current owner or service provider.

Can We Believe The Numbers?

Many Laundromats are 100% cash. It is difficult to verify, with certainty, the true revenue of the location. You have to rely on tax returns, bank statements and the owners' word.

There are Laundromat experts out there who promise they can get you the 'real numbers' by analyzing water bills. Perhaps they can. I can tell you that it is way too easy to fudge water usage and a water bill analysis should be used as a guide at best or to eliminate out and out falsehoods.

For example, an owner can leave a faucet running, not fix a drip or sponsor a car wash to artificially inflate water usage and then, by extension, the unit sales and the business price.

Calculate Max Capacity Revenue

This is just a quick calculation to see where the current owner is reporting his average capacity to be. To calculate this we assume that all the machines are in full operation all day. Figure how many times a machine can operate during posted business hours. Then multiply that number by the machine price. This will give you maximum revenue for that machine for one day.

Do this for all the washers and assume the dryers run continuously. How much money is this and how does it compare to the owners reported daily average revenue?

Example: A top loader in the location you are scouting costs a retail customer $2.00 for each use and runs for 30 minutes per load.

The location is open for 12 hours each day. Max daily revenue for machine is 24 cycles times $2.00 or $48.00 per day.

Let's assume the max revenue for the location you want is $1000 per day. The owner is reporting monthly average gross sales of $15,000. This indicates that he is operating near 50% capacity all day, every day. Spend some time in the business to evaluate it while incognito. Does your observation of the customer traffic support the sellers' claims?

CHAPTER 3- MARKETING

Congratulations! You have purchased your business and now we need to let the world know.

The Laundry industry is a mature industry. You will need to do everything you can to not only lure customers from other Laundromats, but retain your customers as well. Your laundromat should be well lit, clean and all signs should be positive in nature with hours and rules of operation clearly posted

In Store Marketing

Signage

You will need signs in your location to inform customers about your policies and to help protect you and your company against liability. Spend the money to have your permanent signs professionally printed. Don't hand-write any of your signs, not even the 'out of order' ones. This shows your customers that this is a professional establishment with a dedicated owner.

Try to avoid negative tones with your signs. Customers will not feel welcome if every sign says 'NO' such as "NO Smoking," "NO sitting on the equipment," "NO eating," etc. You'll find your customers more willing to follow your rules if you speak to them nicely.

Also try to give them alternatives: For Example, "Please don't sit on the folding tables, we have plenty of seats inside and out."

Be sure to place signs saying that you are not responsible for loss, theft or damage. This will help you in case of frivolous lawsuits.

Be multi-lingual if your neighborhood is. We grew our business by assisting those who spoke primarily Spanish. Our day time attendant was also bi-lingual and the customers loved her. The Spanish speaking customers were only too happy to refer us to their Spanish speaking friends and relatives.

Your in-store signs should also complement your marketing and others services. Do your in-store customers know you have delivery service? Or that you have a web page? Can they contact you via social media? If yes, there should be signage to reflect that.

Clean /Well Lit

A clean, well-lit Laundromat is perceived to be a safe, well run Laundromat. *It behooves you to make yours such.* Word of mouth is still an effective marketing tool and your cleanliness and safety will help drive it.

Proper Layout And Uncluttered

Evaluate your space. Are there enough places to sit? Can customers work comfortably without getting in each other's way? Is there a place for jackets or are they piled up on the folding tables so no one else can use them?

The first Laundromat I bought had lots of excessive furniture. The trashcans were oversized for the space. It had a table for eating, held together with duct tape. The chairs didn't match.

I immediately took everything out, put things back in one at a time until I thought the layout made sense, then tossed the rest.

The business had fewer items, had improved flow and the change really made the lobby area look more open and inviting. It looked more like a Laundromat and less like a second hand furniture store.

Exterior First Impression/ Signs

Many times, new residents to as neighborhood will take a walking tour to check out the new amenities available to them. Will they be impressed with your Laundromat when they walk past it the first time? Will it entice them to walk in and take a look around?

The exterior sign lights should all work and should always be left on when it is dark outside even if you are closed. This is your best method of advertising (in conjunction with your 'van sign"- more on that later)

Window Signs

It is important to have good signage on the front window that gives a quick snap shot of what services you provide, but also does not impede the ability to see in or out.

Use professionally made window decals or go big dollar and have your info and logo imprinted on sunscreen shades which allow customers to see in at night and also out during the day.

Clean Parking Lot

Go outside and look at the front of your store several times a day.

Is it appealing? Pick up trash. Fix broken lights. The cleaner, brighter and, therefore, safer it is the more customers you will attract.

ONLINE MARKETING

Website.

A web presence is a must particularly if you have items that can be purchased online. Customers should be able to print coupons, place delivery orders and buy gift certificates via your web page. Phone number, social media accounts and email address should be on every page.

Social Media

The basics will matter to you. Even if you don't have online items to sell you do want to try communicating to your neighbors and potential customers via social media. Facebook and Instagram posts are free and, if used correctly, can drive sales to your laundromat.

Social Media strategy is an ever-evolving study that I can't do justice here. Please watch tutorials on 'YouTube' if you need assistance with social media strategies.

On Line Directories

No need to pay for specialized listings. 'Yahoo! Local' and 'Google Places' profiles are free and are used by the majority of people searching online.

Flyers, Ads And Handouts

Sometimes old school still works.

Fairs and festivals are great places to wear company t-shirts and pass out flyers or business cards. You also get to enjoy the festival. We had great success obtaining customers by passing out flyers to University students each street fair. Most importantly, we never bought a table.

We did, however, stop at all the tables where we thought the host business could use our services. Make sure you buy something- it helps them pay more attention to your pitch.

Company Vehicle.

Even if you don't have a delivery service, it is very helpful to have a mobile sign. I learned this from a SUBWAY franchisee in Delaware.

He bought the cheapest barely functioning vans he could legally register. They only had to drive to a new parking space on a weekly basis to avoid being towed.

He had the franchise logo professionally painted on the side with an arrow pointing back to the restaurant.

Hundreds of cars passed and saw his location every hour and his sales volume increase dramatically.

Marketing Price Vs. Service

Your Laundry business will compete with one of two strategies: Lowest Price or Best Service.

Competing on Price is a suckers bet in my opinion. You will be under constant pressure to catch bargain hunters with no loyalty and your cash flow will take a hit. It will be difficult to raise prices. You will need to do much more volume to justify the lower price.

Will lowering your prices 25% bring you 30% or more additional daily customers?

Consistent Marketing and providing Best Service is my recommendation to building your best revenues. The key to this strategy is being able to both deliver what you promise, and not being afraid to charge for it.

Best Service means IF you are charging 25 to 50 cents more than your competitors for single washers and at least $1 more for larger capacity washers and dryers, then you MUST...

- Have a store so clean people comment on it.

- The machines should always work and be quickly repaired when they go down.

- Your Attendants must be friendly and helpful.

- Hold the door for people, assist them with moving laundry from washer to dryer (especially if you have people waiting), and carry laundry to and from the customers' car.

Choosing Hours Of Operation

You will need to determine the best hours based upon your specific location.

We opened each day at 7am to get the commuter drop offs for our wash and fold service and to catch a few early birds. We had last wash at 8pm as business dropped off substantially after 9pm in our center and we couldn't justify the expense of an attendant to go much past that on a regular basis.

Your area may vary. It may be well worth going later into the evening or even going 24 hours. If you have a nearby large employer that has a first shift at 6am, it may be worth opening at 5am to get their drop-off business.

Be sure to evaluate the actual cash received by day part for at least the first year to determine your revenue peaks and valleys. If the hourly expenses exceed your hourly revenues for your early or late hours it is obviously not worth being open unless you can effectively market to change that.

I would generally recommend not staying open later than other retail stores in your immediate area. If you have a bar in your strip center, it is not recommended to be open at their closing time as sometimes the inebriated clientele need the restroom or to sit in your chairs watching TV as they wait to sober up and drive home.

This tends to discourage the regular clientele and can make your attendants uncomfortable.

Depending on your lease or space available to you, you can set up a 24 hour drop box for wash and fold. Train your customers to mark their bags to your specifications and they can drop off when you are closed but still pick up on their way home.

What do I promote?

Marketing can be very expensive particularly if you haven't

defined your target customers and most profitable services. We got the best rates of return by promoting the following services.

Comforters For Drop Off Service

Some people only use the Laundromat to wash and dry comforters. They may only do this a few times each year but almost always when the season changes. This is typically when comforters either come out of or go into storage.

Giving a seasonal discount will attract new customers into your location. Once they come in… promote your delivery service or wash and fold service. Always try to upsell your walk-in customers.

Gift Certificates

We have had great success around Mother's Day and Christmas selling gift certificates for our wash and fold service.

We also provided silent auction Gift Certificates for Charities. The Charities raised good money for them and it helped to introduce our service to people we may not have otherwise reached. Many 'bidders' became regular customers.

Clean, Safe And Convenient

Your marketing material should always promote your safety, cleanliness and convenience. Even if it is just a tagline on the bottom of a flyer, it needs to be presented and reinforced in your prospects mind until they associate your location with those three things.

Coupons

Please DO NOT use coupons unless it is for your grand opening, new service promotion or you are trying to compete on price. Many locations will try to entice with 'free dryer days' and frequent user cards. When your place is clean, safe and has proper equipment mix, you will not need to do these things.

Unique Logo

Hire an artist to design a unique logo for the Laundromat. This logo should be used on all things marketing.

That includes business cards, flyers, website, any emails you send out, Facebook and Twitter, etc.

Nothing gets handed out or displayed to your target market without your logo and web address.

Protect your logo and be careful nobody else tries to use it. It is very easy to copy images on the web and laundries from across the country can use it with ease. I know. I was guilty of this until the owner of the art contacted and kindly reminded me that I was violating his copyright.

CHAPTER 4 - MACHINE MIX

A great Laundromat will have the proper equipment mix inside it. While good customer service will help attract repeat business to your store, having the right number of needed capacity machines is crucial to your success. The basic equipment you will need for your Laundromat are washers, dryers, water heaters, change machines, folding tables, laundry carts.

Washers –Large capacity is best.

The bigger washers are your competitive advantage against the apartment building washer/dryer. Most apartments providing washers/dryers are single load (10 lbs) at best and are often smaller double stack style machines.

The average apartment dweller (with children) would rather come over to your laundromat, put a whole week worth of laundry in two or three machines and be done washing, drying and folding in under 2 hours.

Single Washers Top Load Vs. Front Load

Front loaders generally have larger capacity and use a lot less water than top loaders. Your single load machines should be primarily front loaders.

Some customers prefer the top loaders so they don't have to bend as much to load and retrieve their clothes.

Others prefer to leave the lid up to allow clothes to soak a bit before washing. Top loaders are also simpler machines and tend to run longer between repairs and are easier to fix when they do go down.

I compromised by providing two top loaders but I also built custom bases for the single front loaders which raised them six inches higher than they would normally be. This helped to alleviate the bending over issue.

One Dryer Per Every Washer Plus Two More.

There must be capacity balance in your facility. Nothing is worse than having a line for the dryers and having customers walk out to find a dryer somewhere else. If you are big machine heavy (as you should be) you will need at least 2 more 30 lb. (3x) stack dryers than you have individual washing machines unless you have one or two 45 pound stack dryers. The 45 pounders should be reserved for customers using the 6x washer or those drying comforters.

Folding Tables

Try to have at least one folding table for every three dryer pockets. Customers need a place to work. Folding tables don't add revenue per se, but if you are short tables the demand for your location will eventually level down to the point where your folding capacity allows it to be. Most customers fold on site and appreciate the tables as close to the dryers as possible in your location.

If a customer's clothes are dry and there are no folding tables available, several things may happen

-the customer becomes unhappy because they have to wait

-clothes will remain in the dryer while they wait and another customer will have to wait for that dryer and your flow will back up.

-The customer shoves the clothes in a bag and does not come back.

We use four-foot folding tables with shelves. The idea is to fit as many tables in for single use as you possibly can. Bigger tables are nice but customers generally don't like to share and people will try to take a bit of unused table if they are tired of waiting.

Sometimes back-ups cannot be helped. When this happens to you the best thing you can do is to be engaged and do whatever you can to keep your customers happy while they are waiting. This is where your people skills can save the day.

Take charge. Let people know how long they have to wait and assign who is next in what machine so that there are no disagreements or arguments.

The better able you and your staff are at averting a potentially negative situation and making their experience pleasant, the more likely they will want to come back.

Water Heater

It is a cardinal sin in the Laundromat business to not provide hot water.

The size of your water heater depends, of course, on the number of washers you have. Smaller stores (15 washers or less) can work with a 50 gallon household heater anything larger should have at least 100 gallon capacity.

Tankless water heaters are more expensive up front but will save you a small fortune over time in heating and maintenance costs. I encourage installing a tankless system if you will be there for the long haul. Conventional water heaters are fine, but they are more costly to operate over time.

You can, however, tweak your system if you really want to pinch pennies. Turn your temperature down overnight so that you are not keeping hot water while you are closed. Turn it back on ½ hour before you open the next day.

Run lower price points on programmable washers for cold water washes.

CHAPTER 5 -
WASH & FOLD

A good wash and fold service will be a significant source of profit. At current printing, my cost to operate a single washer and dryer per 14 pound load is $1.25. 14 pounds times $1.25 per pound equals $17.50. Gross profit is $16.25.

Subtract your proportional cost of soap, fabric softener, bleach and a dryer sheet (maybe $1.00) and the cost of packaging (another dollar) and you are at $14.25 towards the bottom line.

Compare that to $2.25 for washer and 1.50 average cost per dryer ($3.75 gross minus $1.25 operating equals $2.50 gross profit) and you can see how wash and fold quickly adds to your cash flow and profit.

You can tier your pricing by pounds or frequency to encourage repeat business.

We started doing this when people returning from vacation would bring in around 100 pounds of clothes to be washed and folded but they balked at the $125.00 price tag. I gave them 25% off and still made a $90 profit on the sale. You will not consistently get the big orders if you do not.

Since you are competing on service, be sure to use premium products and keep specialty soaps in stock.

You will need to have non-scented items (Purex), Baby friendly (Dreft), Environmentally friendly, etc. based upon your customers' needs and wants.

Packaging

Wash and fold customers are paying top dollar for your service. Make sure they leave feeling they got their monies worth. Shop around for a pre-printed laundry bag company. There are many and the internet will help you find them. You will need pre-screened nylon bags (which you will sell retail) as well as pre-printed plastic bags specifically designed for square folded laundry.

Nothing looks worse than sending a customer out with a generic plastic trash bag.

Fold By Person

A big customer concern about the wash and fold service is the need to sort clothes after they get them home.

This isn't a big deal for the single customer as everything is theirs, but for two or people mixed together this can be a pain.

Train your regular customers to bring you the clothes already separated by person. By person, not necessarily by color. (If they will do that too, great.) They will greatly appreciate getting it back that way as well.

If the drop is a one-off customer (meaning you may not likely see them again soon) try your best to sort. Mom and Dad's stuff should be easy as should boy and girl clothes. You won't get it perfect but they will appreciate the effort and will remember that when they are in the market for your service again.

Everybody Folds The Same Way

This isn't McDonalds but you should have systems and consistency. This helps to cut down on 'favorite' attendants as tips are largely involved.

Two biggest complaints: t-shirts and socks. Unless you get a specific request for a specific style, everybody gets folded the same way, every time, by each attendant as determined by your best practices.

CHAPTER 6 - STAFFING

Attendants

Your attendants will make or break your repeat business. They must be courteous, helpful and keep the place clean at all times. Customers will gladly give you repeat business if they like your staff as much (or more) as they like your physical operation.

Be sure to give your customers some way to provide feedback to you securely.

Post a phone number or web address for feedback

Have a comments drop box that the staff can't access.

Follow up on all praise and complaints and be sure to give both positive and negative feedback to your staff as well.

Vending/Automation

Please consider using vending machines for as much of your operation as possible to reduce your dependence upon staff. All soap, bags, etc., sold should be vended.

I strongly recommend a bill changer machine to change bills from $20 and $10 to $5 and $1.

Work Programs

We enjoyed working with special needs kids in our Laundromat. The local high school was looking for job training opportunities for higher functioning autistic students and we were able to organize our regular delivery schedule to allow them to come in and fold for us one day per week. This worked for us on a few levels:

The students did receive practical work experience

We built goodwill and positive word of mouth in the community

We did hire several of the students on a part-time basis over the summer for special events.

The school itself became a customer for sports uniforms due to their good experience with us.

CHAPTER 7 – PRICING

Laundries Within 2 Miles

You have to check in on your competition on a regular basis. It's ok. They are going to do it to you. Take notice of what they may be doing better than you. Are any of your former customers there? Are they competing with you on price or service? How do you stack up on an 'apples to apples' comparison? Know what your direct competitors are charging.

You will not make every potential customer happy- some will drive an extra 10 miles (and spend $2.00 in Gas) to not spend the same $2.00 extra in your Laundromat. But if your nearest competitor is across the street, has a nice place, similar machines and is charging less.... You need to do some thinking.

Apartment Building Laundry Rooms

It's ok to be at least 50 cents more per load than apartment building laundry rooms IF you have your place in check. People will spend more to have consistency in working machines, clean/safe environment, something good on TV and a friendly ear to bend.

Apartment building laundry rooms tend to have few machines. They are often located in only one building of a complex and can be an unofficial meeting place for non-tenants. They are often subject to vandalism and are frequently out of order.

Your Competitors.

You need to know what other Laundromats are charging in your immediate area. You should be charging as least as much as they for similar sized machines, more if your location and service is superior. I also subscribe to their blogs, and follow them on Social Media to keep up on any promotions they may be having.

Do not limit yourself to just the local Laundromats. I have 'liberated' many a good idea from Laundromats across the country from the comfort of my own home and laptop.

CHAPTER 8-
ANCILLARY PRODUCTS
& SERVICES

Any space not generating revenue is wasted. If you are at capacity for washers and dryers you need to find some ancillary revenue to maximize your space. Just remember that ancillary revenue is just that and it should not detract, replace or otherwise interfere with your primary business – which is running the best Laundromat in your area.

Ancillary Revenue could be as much as 10% of the Gross Income and makes a big difference to the bottom line. Ancillary items are vending machines, soda and snack machines, video games, pay phones, internet kiosks, tanning beds, massage chairs or anything else you may think of.

The average margin on ancillary revenue sources is around 50 percent, so $1,000 a month of ancillary income would net $500 to the bottom line. The following are what I use in my Laundromats:

Arcade Style Games

Many local amusement companies will lease games for a 50-50 revenue split. This method is easy cash with no upfront or maintenance costs.

You can also find many for sale at reasonable prices should you determine you have sufficient interest in the games. I preferred the lease arrangement as we could switch up the games every few months with no added expense.

Pinball games were very popular in my locations as were cabinet games with multi-game computer boards. We kept the price per game at 25 cents to encourage play. Keep the volume low so that it doesn't interfere with the TV.

Home Gaming Systems

If you have room for it, create a separate space for older model (hence less likely to be stolen) game stations. Rent cartridges and/or controllers by the half hour. Power kill switch behind the counter helps enforcement and renewals.

Vending

Traditional options include snack and soda machines. They need to be in a spot that will not be in direct sunlight and also maintain normal room temperature. Keep them stocked and clean.

Again, this is something that can be outsourced. Many vending companies will provide 100% service and give you a percentage of the proceeds in return. Average percentage is 10-15% of gross revenues per machine.

Higher traffic locations may be able to obtain a video vending machine such as a Redbox.

Transfer Service

A potential added source of revenue for you is the 'transfer service'. Charge customers a dollar to move clothes from the washer to the dryer so they can stay out and complete errands without stopping back in between.

Dry-Clean Drop Off

This works best if you do not have a Dry Cleaning service in your strip mall. Most Leases have a non-compete clause with other tenants anyway and it's also not good for maintaining peer-to-peer friendships. BUT, if they have to make two trips and would prefer to make one, you can be a drop off service for dry-cleaning.

Atm

Only own if you are in a very high traffic area and will get users other than the regular walk-in Laundromat customer.

Lease your ATM with an option to buy if you are not sure what cash flow it will bring in. Do a surcharge split with a vendor if possible just to get a feel for the volume. You can always buy one later.

What Not To Sell

Please keep in mind that you are a Laundromat. You are not...

A tax business

An Avon Lady

Any type of MLM practitioner

Struggling owners will do just about anything to get revenue in the door when times are hard. Focus on your core business and all will be well. This is not to say that you shouldn't or couldn't have side interests. It is simply my recommendation that you not blend everything into one location.

CHAPTER 9 - WHERE NOT TO BE CHEAP

Good operators are always looking for ways to raise revenue and lower costs. You do want to get the best deal you can but do not cut corners in the following areas:

Alarm Systems

Change machines and ATM's are popular targets for break-ins. Be sure to have a monitored Alarm system that will contact authorities for you at 3am should there be mischief.

Wash & Fold Soap And Softener

Use brand name cleaners and promote those names to your customers and prospects. Keep special items that regulars ask for in supply and advertise that you do so.

Special items may include:

Fragrance free soap

Environmentally friendly (no phosphates)

Baby safe

Cleaning Supplies

Always remember, a clean Laundromat is very important towards building your reputation and your word of mouth advertising. Re-stock your cleaning supplies often. Don't let your staff go a single day without having the tools they need to maintain and build your business.

Your Store Appearance

Stay on top of your décor. 'Fancy Fix' any rug tears, chipped tile, broken chairs, etc.

Fanatically clean and dust every day, every shift. Nothing looks less inviting to a potential new customer than duct-taped rugs,

Detail clean the nooks and crannies especially on your machines to keep them looking new.

Customers walking into your location should be greeted with the scent of 'clean', be it pine cleaner, bleach or your favorite surface cleaner.

CHAPTER 10 - WHERE YOU CAN BE CHEAP

Cable Tv Vs Dvd & Radio

I pulled the cable service after a few months of operation in my first Laundromat. It was more because I was cutting back expenses to survive than any flash of brilliance, but the reality was.... DVD's are just as entertaining, don't cost anything after they are acquired, and most people didn't care that we didn't have live TV. Cost per month was changed from $75 to zero.

The changeover was hard at first for the regulars who camped out to watch soap operas and football. But they eventually changed their habits to watch their programming at home. We referred others to the bar down the way while we charged an extra dollar to move their laundry from washer to dryer. We even got a few extra wash and folds out of it during the NFL playoffs.

Radio is also a free service. Customers can't really watch TV while they are folding so some good music is also a good diversion from folding.

Trash

Most Laundromat trash falls into three categories

-Empty soap/fab softener containers

-Discarded clothing

-Cans and wrappers from vending and other miscellaneous trash.

We downsized our commercial trash service by training our customers to separate trash. We provided in store and exterior recycle cans. Plastic soap and bleach bottles, soda cans, cardboard soap boxes, etc. went into one can. Unwanted clothes were placed in a donation bin. Everything else was put into regular trash cans.

We found that about 75% of our 'trash' was either recyclable or able to be donated. We were then able to use a much smaller commercial dumpster to save expense.

Internet

For some reason, Internet service is more expensive for a business than it is for a residence. Not sure why that is…. It just is.

We were fortunate enough to have a neighboring store owner give us the password to his network in exchange for a wash and fold discount. This made sense to us as we could now promote 'Free Wi-Fi' to our customers and provide streaming content to the TV.

If your security system is internet based, it does not make sense to run security cameras, alarm systems or any other sensitive data operations on a shared internet connection. That should always be proprietary with no exceptions.

Spread The Cost Of Vending Soaps

It is well worth trying to get along with some neighboring owners not only to get the scoop on what they are doing, but also to cut expenses on inventory. Vending soaps come in cases of 100 or so depending on the product and can often sit on a shelf for 2-3 months while you whittle down the supply. If you can split a box with another owner, your cash tied up in inventory drops in half. They may even have some supply they can unload on you if you get into a pinch.

Don't be cheap on the quality of your vending product. Keep the vending items all brand names to justify your pricing.

CHAPER 11 -SAFETY AND SECURITY

All monitoring and recording should be disclosed to your staff as a condition of employment and should also be disclosed to your customers. It may even be required by State and Local law. Check with your local authorities to get the statutes for your area.

Cameras

It is always a good idea to be able to monitor your business, regardless of what it is, from a remote location. I strongly recommend you give yourself the ability to see live feed from your location on your PC or smart phone.

Next best is to have a recording system where you have either DVD, VHS or even a computer 'record' each day with your recording device on site.

Last and certainly least preferable are the 'mock' cameras which give the appearance of monitoring. These help keep people in check until somebody needs to see the video and you can't provide it.

Buddy System

Cash businesses are as attractive to thieves as they are to savvy business owners. You can cut your risk of theft by having at least one employee or a few known customers in your location when you cash out your machines. Vary your routine to lessen the odds of an organized stake out and robbery.

If you do cash out at night be sure to have an additional person with you to deter any wrongdoing.

Alarm Systems

Change machines and ATM's are popular targets for break-ins. Be sure to have a monitored Alarm system that will contact authorities for you at 3am should there be mischief. Skim your change machines regularly and at different times to minimize loss if you are hit.

Non- Customers

The unfortunate reality is that you just can't be nice to everybody and there are people you should be on the lookout for. These include:

-Non-customers asking for $100 bill change. Short answer....No. Unless they are a known customer, do not let some random person try to determine how much cash you are holding for change. This is a common method for criminals to determine if you are worth robbing and also is why it is best to have a bill changer to avoid this confrontation.

-Non customers watching TV or waiting for the bus

You need to have a clear policy for everybody. You can't pick and choose amongst the general population for preferential treatment. I discourage loitering but I bend my own rules on bad weather days. I do set a thirty minute limit if not doing laundry as the bus runs every half hour.

Never let anybody loiter just before you are to close.

Can I Use The Bathroom/ Change Machine

I allow anyone to use the restroom or to get change even if they aren't customers today. New residents to the neighborhood will often use this as an excuse to check out your location.

You do need to be aware of anybody who abuses this privilege as some will try to get $100 in quarters for their own business on a Sunday and leave you empty or be hanging out on the corner dealing and using your restroom as a base of operations.

The main thing is to maintain a balance of being a welcoming establishment without allowing a negative element to set up shop.

CHAPTER 12 - RUNNING A DELIVERY OPERATION

Offering pickup and delivery is a natural extension of your wash and fold business and allows you to grow your business to those who wouldn't normally frequent your location. You can enjoy the same high margins (albeit with a few added expenses) and you will be able to attract business that is not within your normal customer zone.

Colleges And Universities

If you are near any colleges or universities with dormitories, your ability to start a profitable delivery operation has just gotten a whole lot easier.

Despite improvements in laundry facilities at our local University, many students there just didn't want to or didn't know how to deal with their laundry. A typical parent's weekend involved a trip to our location with a semester's worth of clothes and an embarrassed parent or two. I would hand them a card, explain our service and a customer was born on the spot. I could often get them to pay for future service the same day.

Word of mouth is a very effective advertising tool. Students tend to be close with those on their floor and certainly their roommates. Each time I got an order from a new building at the beginning of a semester, it would quickly accelerate as word of the service got out.

Expenses will increase as fuel and vehicle maintenance are now a factor.

Business Accounts

Question-What types of businesses use a wash and fold delivery service?

Answer – Any business that is already sending laundry out or is doing it on premise.

• Daycares. Daycares go through all kinds of community clothes, blankets, pillows, toys, crib bedding, etc. Bring business cards and a rate sheet to all the daycares within a 5 mile radius of your Laundromat.

• Nursing Homes/Hospice. I got involved with this through volunteer work. Our Laundromat provided free service to any hospice patient. The doctors, nurses and families really appreciated that and gave us great word of mouth advertising. We also became the outsource provider for a few nursing homes. The home would charge a flat fee to the residents, we did their personal laundry, the Nursing Home paid us directly.

• Hotels/Motels. Most places have their own commercial laundry machines and staff to do the hotels' laundry and won't need your services. BUT. You can become the preferred referral to any guest in need of service. Additionally, should the hotel have a problem with their machines or staff they will come to you to fill in until the matter is resolved. It is worth your time to bring a business card and introduce yourself to all the hotel managers within a 5 mile radius.

• Restaurants. These businesses often send out their aprons, cleaning rags and uniforms.

Knock on doors. Go get business.

Residential Accounts

•   Seniors. I offer discounted service to seniors. Seniors are an excellent source of potential customers as it gets more difficult for them to do household chores as they get on in years. Offering a senior's discount is a very effective way to increase topline sales, still make good margins and also provide a service at a price point that fixed income people are more likely to use.

•   Referrals. Existing customers who referred us to a new, paying customer received $5.00 off their next order. This was successful for us in that it did encourage a bit more word of mouth.

Other Delivery Services

Doing some research on your competitors may be beneficial for both of you. Some Laundry Services do not own the facilities to wash the clothes they pick up. This service is outsourced. You could be that outsource provider.

We did an online search to see who was providing delivery services in our area. There were two other companies at the time. Neither owned their own facilities. We approached both with no initial results. Sometime later one of the companies had a falling out with their provider and they were in a rush to find a new one or else be out of business. We made a deal and have been partnering ever since.

For all other competitors, don't be afraid to do your homework on them. Call your competitors from home and have them pick up your personal laundry one week. Assess what they do well versus what they don't and use what they do well as your own.

Are they easier to get ahold off? Is their pricing comparable? How is the presentation of clothes upon return?

Offering Dry Cleaning

We referred to this in Chapter 8 but in this case we don't care if we have a non-compete clause in our Lease as we are not doing any of the work on site. You can shop around for a dry cleaning partner and most will offer a wholesale rate if you can bring enough business.

We were able to build this business up by attaching our dry cleaning info and pricing to our existing delivery customer receipts.

This is simply a matter of dropping the garments off at a third party dry-cleaner and picking up when ready. Your only expense is time and gas. Your profit is the difference between what the dry cleaner charges you and what you charge to your customer.

Marketing the Delivery Business

Door To Door, Mailers, Flyers

This decision is as much about time versus money as anything.

Door to door will take much more time, but it is the least expensive way to directly target a prospect and you have the benefit of face to face communication. I had some success with this method by targeting the hotels in my area. I went to each one with a flyer and a business card and asked the desk clerk if I could make an appointment with the General Manager to discuss how my service could benefit their business. Be prepared to stay and present your pitch as you will get some immediate meetings. Most times the desk clerk will politely take your stuff and you never hear back. Sometimes you get calls months later for one off deliveries for guests. It's a percentages game. The more people you talk to the more business you will find.

Mailers are quicker but can be very expensive if you don't target only those places that are most likely to do business with you. Don't do mass zip code mailings.

Partnering

We had a deal with a local pizza/sub shop where we cross promoted each other's location. We gave out menus for all customers (especially delivery) and they put our flyers with all of their orders. It was a straight up trade- no cash exchanged. This was beneficial for our delivery business, but not so much for the walk-ins except for comforter drop offs.

Guerrilla marketing never goes out of style and we recommend that you read 'Guerrilla Marketing' by Jay Conrad Levinson.

Logo Vehicle

The least expensive way to get started is getting door magnets and vinyl window lettering. This option gets you a mobile advertising sign for about one hundred dollars.

When you are ready to go all in, it is best to get a vehicle wrap. The vehicle will stand out better and it will look much more professional. The wrap should use the same logo, slogan and colors as your in-store and web marketing.

CHAPTER 13- MAINTENANCE

I strongly recommend that you attend any maintenance workshops that your equipment servicer may provide. Often it is free and the tips you learn and implement will save you money in the long run.

Washer Maintenance

Set up a regular schedule to empty the drain cleanouts on all your washers. You will be amazed at all the items you will find in there. We have found everything from socks to screws to game cartridges. On a good day we find a few dollars in change. Failure to clean on a regular basis will lead to clogging and equipment fail.

Visually inspect belts and hoses for any signs of wear. Do this at least once per quarter. These are typically the easiest of parts to inspect or replace and it is best to do so before they pop and cause a major water spill or put a machine out of order for several days while you wait for the part to come in.

Run your washers empty with approved cleaning solutions to help reduce soap and scum buildup. This will also prevent foul odors from building up in your front loaders.

Check water inlet screens quarterly to prevent buildup. Screen clogs will affect your water flow and may cause valve failure.

Dryer Maintenance

The number one cause of dryer failure for me has been dereliction of lint removal. Clean the primary lint traps daily. Set up a regular schedule to vacuum lint out of every nook and cranny.

Computer boards and coin acceptors need regular cleaning. Use compressed air for a quick clean. NO METALLIC ITEMS are to go near the computer board as you will short it out. Best practice is to unplug your dryers prior to vacuuming and use plastic hoses.

Exhaust vents also need to be cleaned. This is a dirty, pain in the butt job, but it is also very critical. Your dryers need proper air draft to the outside. There are air regulating flaps within your exhaust vents that prevent air blow back. Should these be blocked either open or shut due to lint, your dryers will malfunction.

Hop up on the roof every now and then to make sure birds haven't nested in your vents to stay warm over the winter. Nests will block air flow, especially if they fall inside. Screen off your roof top vents, if they are not already, and clean the screens of lint on a regular basis.

CHAPTER 14 - COINS VS PRE-PAID CARD OPERATIONS

I've never used card acceptors in my operation. I did, however, accept many customers from other Laundromats who didn't like the card system and preferred our coin-op. There are, however, pros and cons to each.

Coins

Pros – Everybody has full access to them from multiple sources.

'Extra' coins can be spent elsewhere in the Laundromat.

Cons – Need to maintain a change machine.

Cash in store increases probability of Robbery.

Non-customers removing coins from premises.

Pre-Paid Cards

Pros – helps build customer loyalty

Removes majority of cash from premises

Owner is 'pre-paid' for services even if not used.

Cons – Customer perception of balance 'theft' if policy is to not refund unused balance. Increased expense for readers and balance loaders

Attendants need access to card software for refunds

There are hybrid acceptors that allow for both coin and credit card operation of the washers and dryers. This may be a viable option for you. Consult with your equipment provider for more details.

CHAPTER 15 – FINAL COMMENTS

Your success in the laundry business will boil down to the following summary items:

-Buying/Building at the best price

-Providing excellent customer service

-Maintain cleanliness

-Maintain working equipment

-Be involved in your business

Please don't be the type of owner that shows up every now and again just to refill the change machines. Take interest in your daily affairs and the business will take care of you.

I sincerely wish you the best of luck in opening your own Laundromat. Please feel free to contact me via e-mail at info@udlaundry.com with any questions or comments regarding the information in this book.

You can also find some very good information and

additional links at the following websites:

www.planetlaundry.com

www.coinlaundry.org

www.americancoinop.com